T0130504

Lovely Random Thoughts

Poems by Ann Colvin

Order this book online at www.trafford.com
or email orders@trafford.com

Most Trafford titles are also available at major online book retailers.

Printed in the United States of America.

ISBN: 978-1-4269-6641-5 (sc)

Trafford rev. 04/16/2011

 www.trafford.com

North America & international
toll-free: 1 888 232 4444 (USA & Canada)
phone: 250 383 6864 ♦ fax: 812 355 4082

This Book Is Dedicated To

Jean Wood

My sis who loving, "Stays on my butt!"

CONTENTS

Affectionately

WASTED WORDS

It's important for me to tell you,
For I'm so eager for you know,
The moment just after waking
Is the best time for you to show.

Unmeasured care to loved one
So don't waste time to sew
Those little seeds of proverbs
To help your love life grow!

Don't waste your time in silence
Unspoken words are unheard
That's why my friend I'm pleading
Speak up at the slightest urge.

And those friends you see so often
Who could use uplifting words
Just a little bit of console,
Like the chirrup of a bird.

Oh, my friend, please start sharing,
Inexpensive loving lore.
For I speak from my own inertness
Now alone with words galore

That's stacked, unused, and cluttered
Just lying on my floor.
Wasted love that's now useless
Loving words, used nevermore.

For my love one gone forever
Not to walk through my front door.
For he only lives in memories.
As he's with God forevermore.

WHAT'S WRONG?

What's wrong with us loving
From our very first sight?
It doesn't take a lifetime
For our love to be just right.

What's wrong with us laughing
Over a little incident?
A moment in time captured
Joyous fun, before life's spent.

What's wrong with us living
In our tranquil atmosphere?
Enjoying all life offers
With easy comfort. Without fear?

What's wrong with disagreements?
It helps to clear the air.
Make up later is worth it,
There in our lovers lair.

What's wrong with being stubborn
When living a life with you?
Staying with you is no question.
Know you feel that same way too.

What's wrong with us sharing
Every moment of the day?
A grasp of joyous pleasure
Makes everyday a perfect day!

What's wrong in giving fantasies,
To my very special love?
Just a way of thanking God,
For our love, a treasure trove

What's wrong with growing older
With my love. A valid treat!
Together gathering memories
Makes our journey so complete?

To my sweet hubby--gone but not forgotten

WORDS

Love words spoken,
Loyal, devoted.
Words that you share!

Angry words spoken
Infuriate rage.
Wrath without care.

Words of disclosure,
Literal. Precise.
Revealing all you dare.

Words chosen wisely,
Lingering. Emergent.
Descriptive words you bare.

TO MY CHILDREN

My heart is very heavy
I can't explain it all.
There's so much I want to tell you,
Words aren't at my beck and call.

There's so much space between us
And I can't fathom why.
If only we were talking but,
Precious minutes rushes by.

Well, some day you will be here
Wanting your child to explain,
All their pain and hurtful feelings,
While you're frozen in unknowing shame.

I pray with your gained knowledge
You in time will comprehend
That, my love for you is endless
I'm gone, but child love never ends!

5/5/09

Sharing

LET'S GO HUNT'IN BEAR

I thought of you as Godly
Trust your every word.
I'd do anything you tell me
Even if it is absurd!

No idea you'd ever trick me,
But you enjoy the leader roll
Rule of my life freely given
Having fun was your main goal.

You say no harm intended
Just a simple statement said.
You say you didn't plan it.
Just popped into your head.

You insist there's no point
To fool me with your word
I just listened TO intently
My judgment clearly blurred,

An invitation given
Simply, "Let's go hunting BEAR,"
But I stand here so embarrassed,
You just stand there and stare.

Next time you do the invite,
Please spell it out real clear.
Do you want us with our clothes on,
Or both of us go BARE?

1/1/07

IM SO LUCKY TO BE, THE LUCKEST ME.

My heart is bursting with majestic bliss.
I just walked into my imagined wish.
This feeling --the essence of a first kiss.
A feeling by chance I nearly missed.
I'm so lucky to be, the luckiest--ME!

I'm caught up in this golden beam,
The sky's so blue, the air is so clean.
For this dream is the most incredible dream.
A dream that took a lifetime to glean.
I'm so lucky to be, the luckiest-- ME!

I'm floating in a whipped cream sea.
How can this be given to me?
If this is a dream-please don't wake me!
For my God is smiling freely on me.
I'm so lucky to be the luckiest--ME!

For come true dreams are extremely rare!
Ultimate dreams are for those who dare.
My dream came true because you care.
A dream that's big enough to share
I'm so lucky to be the luckiest—ME

HOLIDAY WORKERS

To all of the tireless persons
Who never seem to fail,
To keep this country moving
We must give a hearty hail!

Doctors and nurses
Their lives they've lent us.
Grocers and newscasters,
Service station attendants,

Fire fighters, Policemen
Pilots and crew
Always there waiting
To do service for you.

Then there's the Farmers
Who deserve honorable label.
Lest we forget our military
Making our country stable.

Then there's the steadfast
Homeless shelter saints
And Salvation dinner servers,
All with joy, no complaints.

Phone operators, baby sitters,
For all of those that work.
Cab drivers, and waiters
Who puts up with us jerks.

Water and gas men
Electrician too
Emergency stand bys
To repair things for you

TV repair men
Most important of all.
Can't do one holiday
Without our football.

And don't forget Moms
Or the love ones who,
Made all this lovely dinner
For me and you and you!

Making our holidays happy
And so smooth for all of us,
And doing it so thoroughly,
Without the slightest fuss

All personnel unmentioned,
No harm was ever meant!
Your work is as important
Thanks is still our sincere intent.

When will we start thinking
Past our own environment
To simply give a thank you,
To those so diligent?

We say a GREAT BIG 'THANK YOU',
To those across our land
Hopping thanks is sufficient
For you taking your great stand.

GOD Bless YOU ALL,
        HAPPY HOLIDAYS,
                AND AGAIN, THANK YOU! 11/27/09

How To Say--"THANK YOU"

Of all the things in this big world
The toughest thing to do,
To all our friends or relatives
To say a big "THANK YOU!"

Oh, we hem and haw, and mumble,
Saying words of some value.
All we really need to express
Is a most sincere: THANK YOU!"

But we ease our minds by sending
A gift tied up in blue,
Thinking we've tactfully done our best
And that's all we need to do.

But the simplest thing in this big world
Too simple for us to do,
Is to take the love one close to our heart And simply say,
    "THANKS! I LOVE YOU!"

Spiritual

WHY GOD?

Why do we have mean people God?
That inflicts pain, and give the devil a nod?
Who always thinks on the sad side of life?
Do they really enjoy so much trouble and strife.

Stealing all happiness, prolonging fear.
Taking our joy, as their evil rears!
I know Your allowing Your bad and good
Giving us options to do as we should

To give us our choice, of evil or love.
Your heart's overjoyed looking down from above For most
of your children enjoys your pleasure.
Evil ones defeated. They lost all your treasures.

It's sad they don't know the choice we're given
With our reward, a mansion in heaven.
They're made an example with their non respect
Their mansions in Hell with that pyromaniac

11/28/2009

THANK YOU GOD

Standing below majestic mountains,
Looking across the grassy plains
Enjoying the mighty oceans
Or waving fields of golden grain

When we think of things that trees do
Holding nests on their strong limbs
And giving squirrels a daily workout
As if trees are their private gym.

Looking at a orange sunset
Feeling rain upon your face
Seeing first snowflake of winter
Confirm this land is a great place

GOD'S WHISPER

Listen closely for GOD'S WHISPER
Listen to hear the gentle sound.
A nudging whisper or suggestion,
Completed answers will abound!

When God whispers, It's so quiet.
Mistaken often for self will.
Acting on his words of wisdom
Cures all threatening evil ills.

Faith and trust, is all He ask for,
To hear the answers from above.
Belief will grow with each submission.
From His warm and tender love.

So let belief in Him assure you.
Let the struggles of life just leave,
Into the hands of blessed Comfort
when God's blessings are bequeath

Faith and trust comes so easy,
Hard to believe--but very true.
Examine the process of surrender.
Almost to easy for us to do!

Dedicated to my wonderful son Frank!
Who listens and hears Gods whisper--
And who taught me to listen!

Love Mom,
Ann Colvin
March 29, 2008

Children

MY BOUNCING BALL

MY ball bounces up so high
It bounces up to touch the sky!
Sometimes my friend comes out to play.
We have fun. I hope she'll stay.

But the ball bounces into her yard,
Her mother sees her, says in a stern word,
"Time for dinner. Go wash your hands."
She always does what her mother commands.

But my ball is still
 In her front yard.
All playing is stopped.
Ball bouncing is barred.

But tomorrow being another day,
Maybe then she'll come out to play.
We'll bounce the ball and jump and run.
Just bouncing ball is so much fun.

March 31, 2009

WHY?

Why are babies made so small ?
So helpless and so sweet
But they have this great big problem
Cant walk or even speak

With big round eyes, curly hair
And rosy dumpling cheeks.
That's how God makes very sure
They're loved from head to feet!

And that's why they're so tiny.
So precious and so pink.
Makes us want to hold them.
But, wow! Can they make a stink!

July 1, 2007

It's All About Me!

DILEMMA, DILEMMA

Oh dilemma, dilemma,
Which way do I go?
This way or that way
Oh, who's to know?

The question's so pressing
Time's is at hand.
To give forth the answers
Is life's big demand.

Weigh both sides carefully
So many pros and cons
Before I give an answer
Need to be sure it's the right one.

7/13/08

MY CATCH 22

I should be rich but,
My mind's is a blank
New inventions are lost.
Because I simply can't think.

Lord, I sit and wonder,
Who could love this mindless bore.
I would ask for your help,
But, what do I ask for?

So, I suppose my prayer is,
Not being to absurd
'Is to simply ask for brains,
If I could only find the words.'

September 4, 2007

NEAR PERFECTION

Perfection is not possible,
Only one could that achieve!
The goal is in the trying.
Near perfection if you believe.

We show the world daily,
Exactly what we're about.
I'm sure our words and actions,
Express our goal, no doubt!

We are given only one life.
What we do is our own choice.
Near perfection gives us freedom.
Achieving gives us our voice.

The shame is when our path is known
And our goals becomes clear visions,
By then we cannot win life's race
From a back starting position.

November 16, 2009

OOOPS OR IS IT JUST ME?

Today is gloomy--dull--unbright
Stinky- irritating, nothing is right
Don't want you to talk to me ,
Or even crack a smile
I don't even want to see you,
Or I'll go into exile.
Don't play your happy music
Your funny jokes can go.
No flowers, or pets, or Candies.
Please! You busy so and so!
Just leave me here to ponder
All the gloom and misery.
Why are you so depressing?
Or could it possibly be--
                    Just me?

                              5/5/08

WHO'S RESPONSIBLE

I stand alone
*   As only I can.*
In this situation
*   I've got myself in.*

Remembering back
*   To the very first,*
Or was it the hundredth time
*   Mother's temper burst.*

When she's faced
*   With my creations,*
For me exploring
*   All life's elations*

In the end
*   For all my actions*
The negative outcome
*   Of my contraptions.*

There's just one thing
*   When I get sane*
I'm the one and
*   only one to blame*

12-27-2007

..*Animals*

MY DOG'S PERPECTIVE

You think I've got it easy,
But you need to think again!
I lay here waiting patiently
For our lovely day to begin.

Let's start off with our mornings,
Oh! for sure that's a bore.
You go fix yourself breakfast,
After you shove me out the door!

And now your breakfast's over
I think 'It's my turn to eat!'
But you go get yourself ready,
While I lay here at your feet.

Then you buzz around so frantic
Not thinking what my life's about.
Seems like wasted motion.
But to you there is no doubt.

It's something you call "Work".
This I don't quite understand.
But that's why you're so flustered.
I say, "make a better plan!"

Out the front door you go flying.
I'm hoping you'll come back in.
So I lye down by it waiting
For our fun day to begin

I sleep--I wake--and turn over.
A million times I'd say.
Finally the front door opens
You say, "I've had a rotten day!"

You fix yourself a sandwich,
A salad, and a drink.
You don't even stop to ask me
"Whatever do you think?"

Oh you give me that ole' dry stuff
Tasteless, boring, and really flat.
I know you would never touch it.
And I want to give it back.

What's this you're getting ready
You think that I don't know
That routine that you go through
Just again before you go.

This could be a very long night
Another long night alone.
I wish you'd turn on the T.V.
To drown out that ringing phone.

So you think leading a Dog's life
Is such a lovely sport.
Think again my selfish partner,
It's lonely and boring, I retort!"

MY BEST FRIEND

Your eyes are understanding
So big and round and bright.
You listen so intently,
Though my words aren't just right!

Your aura is so consuming,
With your magnetic love appeal.
You're always there just waiting
With immeasurable good will.

Let me be the first to tell you,
Of my undying gratitude.
For you are the best PET ever,
With your steadfast attitude!

5/5/2009

PLEASE DEAR, I WANT A CAT!

Sitting alone in my lounger
With the same thought again today
I had to get my courage up
Cause I have something vital to say

"I want a cuddly cat. I said!
My mind is already set!
I know what you are going say,
We're too old for a little pet."

"Oh hubby, how can you take care
Of a frisky mischievous cat?
You know there's lots work involved
And you know who'd get that!

You see the man's diabetic
Lost a leg. Don't go much now
That's why a little playful pet
Would give his life some-WOW

He'd keep me company all day long
And take my mind off things
He'd pounce around playfully
With the endless joy he'd bring

She knew that anticipation
Made his want grow so much stronger
So she gave a "put off" answer
Forcing his wait--a little longer

Don't try to change my mind dear
He'd lie quietly on my lap.
Why cant you enjoy the fun with me
With an adoring loving cat

Although his wife understood
And wanted to give in
The value of the cat would grow
Not complying to his first whim

So the man got down on his one knee
Begging and pleading still
Can't you possibly see that beautiful cat
Curled up on our window sill.

With that, the wife had no defense
She might as well give in
Oh ok, she finally said,
You always knew you'd win.
(TRUE STORY)   12/14/2009

GATES

Gates have a purpose!
Open to pass through.
Closed gates are for keeping.
I'm sure you already knew.

This gate is for Keeping,
My buddy, best friend--My pet!
So my friend if you open-
Then close it and,
        please don't forget!

(NOTE: THIS WAS WRITTEN BECAUSE MY YARD IS FENCED, AND
EVERYONE DOES NOT KNOW HOW TO CLOSE A GATE! SO I MADE
THIS AS A SIGN TO ADORN ALL MY GATES.....)

EXCUSE ME, I'M A LADY

I'm little but I'm mighty
Red, Orange, yellow, or brown
With speckles scattered on my back
Very colorful and round

I'm a simple little mama,
Love my children I contend.
I always love and care of them
Least it's said by all my friends.

Why are they always yelling
For me to go back home?
Excuse me, I'm a lady
Don't have time to roam

Saying my house is on fire
They call me "Lady Bug."
Yes I'm a lady all the way
But I think they've hit the jug.

For when I got home all I saw
Is children running about
House not burned. They're not alone
Why would they all cry out?

Editables

RECIPE FOR LOVE
(song)

I don't want chocolate in my bowl of hot chili.
Don't want tamales in my blue berry pie.
Don't want pears in my dish of spaghetti,
But thinking of you gives my heart butterflies.

I don't want honey on my cheese quesadilla,
Don't like mustard in my bowl of beef stew.
I don't want nuts in my banana pudding.
But my hearts all a twitter just thinking of you.

Burgers and fries,
Carrots and peas
Ice cream and cake
Crackers and cheese.
Just you and me, together we'd be
A great combination, throughout eternity.

I don't need peas in my bowl of peach cobbler,
Don't want doughnuts with tomatoes and such.
I don't want Jell-O in creamy mashed potatoes
But a dash of sweet lovin' is just the right touch

I don't want celery in my cup of hot cocoa.
Don't want cheese on my favorite cake
I don't want jam in my fresh Caesar Salad
Together with you, Oh the music we'd make.

Burgers and fries,
Carrots and peas
Ice cream and cake
Crackers and cheese.
Just you and me, together we'd be
A great combination, throughout eternity.

COFFEE DOESN'Y TASTE LIKE COFFEE ANYMORE
(song)

Got up in the morning
Went to the door
That's when I first noticed
My bare feet on the cold floor.

Need to get my coffee
To wake myself up.
Hope that you've made it
And we have a clean cup!

Now to get myself some breakfast
Makes my morning so complete
What's that? We've only cereal
Now, just isn't that a treat?

Then I take a sip of coffee
And fall down on the floor.
Cause my coffee doesn't taste
like coffee anymore.

They have brewed, and stewed
and freeze dried
My favorite morning drink
So I ask you to try it!
To see what you might think.

I can see in your eyes, asking
What are you thinking Dear?
Why did you make me drink this drink?
It taste worse than stale beer!

I ask you "What is in it?
Is that nuts all crunched up?
And I don't like all this foam
On top of my coffee cup!

And leave out the Aamaretto
Hazel nut, and or Mudslide
French Vanilla, or Kahluaa
How do you get all that inside?

A Chocolate Almond Toffee
What? Is coffee crunchy now?
Special Blends are so numerous
Bean growers please take a bow"

Gotta get a cup of coffee
Plain and simple cup will do
All that stuff makes me so weary.
For the junk you put me through!

So, I take sip of coffee
Again fall to the floor
Cause my coffee doesn't taste
Like coffee any more.

12/6/2009

DIET

Oh how I love pizza
And cakes
And pasta too

They tell me they aren't healthy
Very fattening,
Vein clogging Oooo/

But I will die so happy
Gaining weight,
Fast heart attack.

You will die as quickly
Thin, attractive,
And that is that!

Not The End

...